the

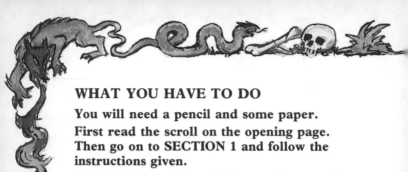

WHAT YOU HAVE TO DO

You will need a pencil and some paper.

First read the scroll on the opening page. Then go on to SECTION 1 and follow the instructions given.

You will then make a dangerous journey, but YOU will decide what paths to follow. On your way you will have to solve clues that spell out a message for Steeleye the Raven.

If you choose the right paths, and if you solve the mysterious clues correctly, your message will describe a creature whose name Steeleye must discover if he is to save the dying valley.

Acknowledgments:
Game plan devised by Roger Hurt. The publishers would also like to thank Joan Collins for her help in making this book.

British Library Cataloguing in Publication Data

Kingsley, Jason
    Steeleye and the lost magic.—
    (Adventure gamebook).
    1. Adventure games—Juvenile literature
    I. Title   II. Davis, Jon   III. Series
    793'.9   GV1203
    ISBN 0-7214-0996-2

First edition

Published by Ladybird Books Ltd Loughborough Leicestershire UK
Ladybird Books Inc Lewiston Maine 04240 USA

Printed in England

COMPETITION BOOK

STEEL EYE
and the
LOST MAGIC

written by JASON KINGSLEY
illustrated by JON DAVIS

Ladybird Books

FOR ENTRY FORM AND PRIZE DETAILS TURN TO BACK PAGE

Once upon a time there was a valley where the sky was always blue. Birds sang in the green trees, and clouds of butterflies danced over the summer flowers.

On the hillside above, a crystal spring bubbled up through the grass. This was the Spring of Joy and it fed an enchanted stream that watered the valley and brought it life and happiness.

Close by lived the guardian of the Spring, an old, old wizard. Each dawn he chanted words of magic in his cracked old voice, and the enchanted stream continued to dance and sparkle in the sunlight.

But one day the wizard fell sick and died. No longer were the magic words spoken every morning, and the Spring began to fail. The valley became parched and dry. The trees and plants and flowers lost their strength and died. Most of the birds and butterflies flew away.

The heart of the land ceased to beat.

1 But the Great Grey Raven stayed on in the valley. His name is **Steeleye**. He is older than the valley itself, but there is still fire in his eyes as he circles over the valley and the forest beyond it. He is searching for the **Hero of Destiny** who will one day come over the mountains to help to find the lost magic that can give back life to the dead valley.

For an ancient legend of the valley tells of a creature who learned from the wizard the secret words of the lost magic; and it prophesies that one day a child, brave and determined, will discover who this creature is. Then Steeleye will travel to the ends of the earth, if he must, to learn the secret for himself.

Many heroes arrive, hoping to aid Steeleye in finding the lost magic. When you opened this book and began to read, **YOU** became one of them.

At this moment, Steeleye the Great Grey Raven is perching above you on the branch of a withered oak tree. He is croaking a message to you in his harsh voice.

If you want to understand his message, you must TURN to 42. Listen **carefully** to what Steeleye tells you. His words will help you to discover a secret message. It will enable Steeleye to recover the lost magic of the valley.

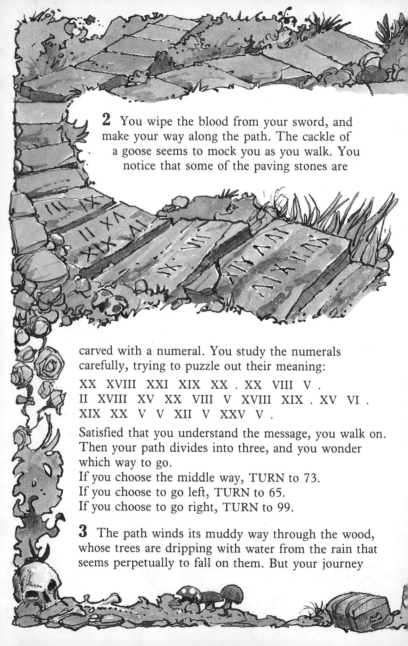

2 You wipe the blood from your sword, and make your way along the path. The cackle of a goose seems to mock you as you walk. You notice that some of the paving stones are

carved with a numeral. You study the numerals carefully, trying to puzzle out their meaning:

XX XVIII XXI XIX XX . XX VIII V .
II XVIII XV XX VIII V XVIII XIX . XV VI .
XIX XX V V XII V XXV V .

Satisfied that you understand the message, you walk on. Then your path divides into three, and you wonder which way to go.

If you choose the middle way, TURN to 73.
If you choose to go left, TURN to 65.
If you choose to go right, TURN to 99.

3 The path winds its muddy way through the wood, whose trees are dripping with water from the rain that seems perpetually to fall on them. But your journey

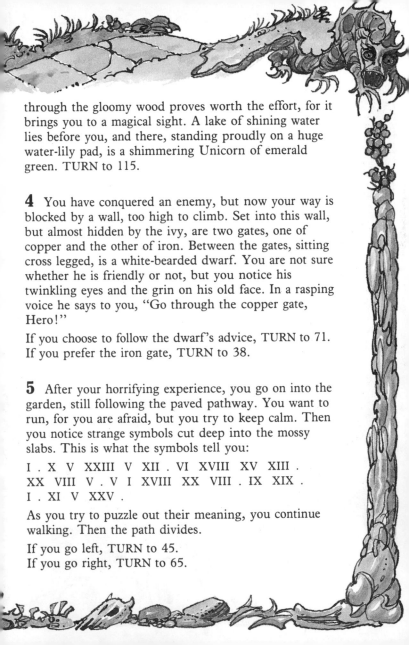

through the gloomy wood proves worth the effort, for it brings you to a magical sight. A lake of shining water lies before you, and there, standing proudly on a huge water-lily pad, is a shimmering Unicorn of emerald green. TURN to 115.

4 You have conquered an enemy, but now your way is blocked by a wall, too high to climb. Set into this wall, but almost hidden by the ivy, are two gates, one of copper and the other of iron. Between the gates, sitting cross legged, is a white-bearded dwarf. You are not sure whether he is friendly or not, but you notice his twinkling eyes and the grin on his old face. In a rasping voice he says to you, "Go through the copper gate, Hero!"

If you choose to follow the dwarf's advice, TURN to 71.
If you prefer the iron gate, TURN to 38.

5 After your horrifying experience, you go on into the garden, still following the paved pathway. You want to run, for you are afraid, but you try to keep calm. Then you notice strange symbols cut deep into the mossy slabs. This is what the symbols tell you:

I . X V XXIII V XII . VI XVIII XV XIII .
XX VIII V . V I XVIII XX VIII . IX XIX .
I . XI V XXV .

As you try to puzzle out their meaning, you continue walking. Then the path divides.

If you go left, TURN to 45.
If you go right, TURN to 65.

6 Your senses are screaming *'Danger!'* Then, in the silence, you hear a low howl followed by a sniffing noise. Cautiously, making as little noise as possible, you take Gorin from its scabbard. Suddenly a monstrous shape looms up before you, its eyes glowing with white fire. It makes a leap for your throat, but Gorin's keen edge easily slices through the monster's neck. Yet the beast does not die! It gives an unearthly howl and gradually fades from sight. On the ground before you lies a red amulet, and you quickly realise that the beast had been wearing it round its neck. Gorin has cut through the cord! You wonder whether to leave the amulet lying there, or to pick it up and examine it. TURN to 85.

7 Further on, the way is strewn with small pebbles of different colours. Then the path divides. On one of the paths there are black and white pebbles. The other is covered with smooth green grass.

If you choose the pebbly path, TURN to 12.
If you choose the grassy path, TURN to 60.

8 Your leg is burning with pain. Gritting your teeth, you pull a barbed arrow from your thigh and at once the sharp pain ceases. You look more closely at the arrow. On its shaft are some spidery brown letters that spell out a mysterious message:

"Spin bury around a bit, and you have a gem of a word."

Surely this instruction will help towards finding the lost magic! Or is it a trick? As you walk on, trying to solve the arrow's message, the path curves round a thicket of silver birch trees. Two muddy paths are leading in different directions into the woodland.

If you follow the right-hand path, TURN to 51.
If you follow the left-hand path, TURN to 41.

9 Sitting down on a fallen tree trunk, you unfold the parchment and begin to study it. On it are written the following strange words:

"Words hide initially. This enigma boldly emphasises a rule. Do learn its eventful secret."

What are the words that 'hide', you wonder? Still puzzling it out, you walk on until you reach a forest clearing. Five paths lead out of it, and you must take one of them. But which?

You want to stay to think about the message, but you know that time is short, and you must hurry on.

If you choose the nearest path, TURN to 37.
If you choose the second one, TURN to 53.
If you choose the third, TURN to 101.
If you choose the fourth, TURN to 14.
If you head for the one farthest off, TURN to 74.

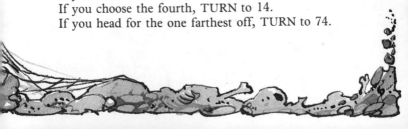

10 The staircase, decorated with delicately carved birdshapes, leads upwards in a dizzying spiral. You begin to climb, and halfway up you notice that each step in the staircase is carved with a numeral. You race back down and study the carvings as you ascend for a second time. This is what you find:

I XVII XIV XIX VII IV XVII XVIII . XIV V .
XVIII XIX IV IV XI IV XXIV IV . XXVI XVII IV .
VI XX VIII III VIII XIII VI . XXIV XIV XX .

Then the sequence is repeated again and again until you have reached the top of the stairs, so you have plenty of time to work out its meaning. TURN to 26.

11 The path narrows as it enters a damp wood, and soon it peters out altogether. The ground begins to rise steeply, and you pull yourself up using the roots of trees as hand and footholds. But at the very top of the incline you lose your grip. You find yourself slithering down a muddy slide, and it is taking you towards a sparkling lake. When you have stopped sliding you pick yourself up, and catch your breath in sudden wonder. For facing you, standing on a huge lily pad that floats upon the water, is a huge emerald-green Unicorn. TURN to 115.

12 It is soon difficult going, however, because the path becomes overgrown with thick, coarse grass. Eventually you reach a high, ivy clad wall. Sitting between two gates set into the wall is a white-bearded dwarf. One gate is of wood, the other of bronze. You approach the dwarf cautiously, wondering if he is friendly. He grins at you, and his eyes are twinkling merrily as he says, "I'd advise you to go through the wooden gate. Wood is wise, whilst bronze is only good."

If you take the dwarf's advice, TURN to 54.
If you choose the bronze gate, TURN to 43.

13 The stairs lead upwards. Is it your footsteps that are making a scuffling on the wooden boards, or is it something else? A terrible fear suddenly descends upon you. TURN to 26.

14 Before long, the way you have taken becomes soggy, and your feet sink deeper and deeper into the boggy ground. Your heart gives a sudden lurch! Something has you caught by the ankle. TURN to 39.

15 The darkness is total, and you have no means of finding your way forward. Then you remember the Unicorn's tear. As you hold it in your hands, a flame begins to glow within it, and soon the whole chamber is lit by its clear, pale blue light. You can now see that five dark tunnels lead out of the pit you are in. But they are set high up, and you must climb to reach them.

If you choose to clamber up to the first one, TURN to 104.
If you go for the second tunnel, TURN to 92.
If you prefer the third, TURN to 84.
If you try to reach the fourth, TURN to 108.
But if you choose the fifth, the highest of all, TURN to 112.

16 You step onto dry land again, and approach the castle gateway. The ground begins to tremble and out of the castle strides a fearsome Dragon. His scales flash, his terrible claws dig up the ground as he moves, and the flames from his nostrils scorch everything in his path. He rears up before you, spreading his mighty crimson wings, and roars his message:

"I am the Guardian of the Gate!" he bellows. "State your business! Be brief, or be gone!"

You answer, "I am searching for the heart of the land. The Unicorn told me I'd find it in the castle!"

At the mention of the Unicorn, the Dragon steps aside. "Pass, friend!" he says courteously.

There are two dark passageways into the castle.

Do you take the left-hand passage? Then TURN to 22.
Do you take the right-hand passage? Then TURN to 30.

17 You realise that the high chamber is filled with the green foliage of a single tree, whose great bark-covered trunk is thick with age. Then you hear the sound of a rich, rustling voice: "I am Green Leaf," it says, "and I am Yellow Leaf! I am the whole Life of the forest. I am the King!"

You kneel before the huge tree, awed by the majesty into whose presence you have come. But the King's lined face breaks into a twiggy smile. "Do not be afraid!" he says. "I shall not harm you. You have come so far to help Steeleye find the lost magic! Climb to the roof of the tower, and speak what has to be spoken!"

If you climb up yourself to a window in the high chamber, TURN to 59.
If you allow yourself to be lifted by the King, TURN to 114.

18 The lead tube crumbles to dust at your touch. But it had contained a rolled sheet of thin silver, and this is unharmed. Smoothing it out, you see that the message it bears has become tarnished, and parts of it are illegible. All you can make out are the words:

"...is true. For the plan... foiled... lost. Hero dead in minutes."

You search the desk for more clues, but there is nothing. Closing the desk top, you walk towards the door. Outside is a landing.

If you decide to go left along it, TURN to 88.
If you go right, TURN to 76.

19 Confronting you now is a fearsome troll, its skin covered in flaking scales, its ugly body tufted with clumps of wiry hair. You make a desperate attempt to draw Gorin, but the troll's great fist slams into your jaw and you are knocked backwards by the force of the blow. But this gives you precious time in which to draw your sword. With one sweep of its mighty blade you cut off the troll's head. To your amazement, the corpse disappears, and lying in its place is a blue amulet. TURN to 90.

20 With a sigh of relief, you reach the shore and once more set foot on dry land. You make for the castle that lies directly ahead, but there is a sudden clattering of hooves. A strange creature, half man and half horse, gallops up to you.

"I am the Guardian of the Gate!" says the Centaur. "State your business!"

"I am searching for the heart of the land," you answer, "and I am told it lies within this castle."

The Centaur throws back his noble head and gazes into your eyes. It seems satisfied with what it sees, for it says, "Pass, friend!"

Set into the castle wall you see a heavy, iron-bound door. Beside it is a flight of worn steps, and next to them a passage.

If you decide to go in by the door, TURN to 86.
If you decide to climb the steps, TURN to 105.
If you go down the passage, TURN to 30.

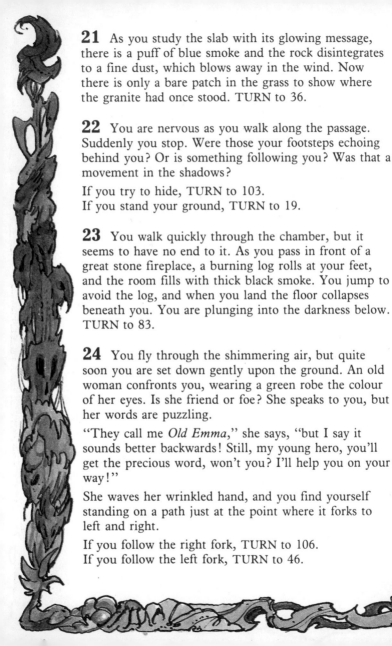

21 As you study the slab with its glowing message, there is a puff of blue smoke and the rock disintegrates to a fine dust, which blows away in the wind. Now there is only a bare patch in the grass to show where the granite had once stood. TURN to 36.

22 You are nervous as you walk along the passage. Suddenly you stop. Were those your footsteps echoing behind you? Or is something following you? Was that a movement in the shadows?

If you try to hide, TURN to 103.
If you stand your ground, TURN to 19.

23 You walk quickly through the chamber, but it seems to have no end to it. As you pass in front of a great stone fireplace, a burning log rolls at your feet, and the room fills with thick black smoke. You jump to avoid the log, and when you land the floor collapses beneath you. You are plunging into the darkness below. TURN to 83.

24 You fly through the shimmering air, but quite soon you are set down gently upon the ground. An old woman confronts you, wearing a green robe the colour of her eyes. Is she friend or foe? She speaks to you, but her words are puzzling.

"They call me *Old Emma*," she says, "but I say it sounds better backwards! Still, my young hero, you'll get the precious word, won't you? I'll help you on your way!"

She waves her wrinkled hand, and you find yourself standing on a path just at the point where it forks to left and right.

If you follow the right fork, TURN to 106.
If you follow the left fork, TURN to 46.

25 The path you have chosen goes through a tunnel formed by the tall rose bushes. Overhead, clusters of orange coloured grapes are hanging from their vines, and you look at them thirstily. But as you move to pick some, a giant white rabbit, brandishing a double headed axe, springs into your path. You open your mouth to speak to him.

"Deeds, not words!" he snarls, and lunges at you with the axe. You dodge the blow and wrench Gorin from its scabbard. The rabbit strikes again, but you catch him off balance and knock him over with the flat of your sword. Before he can recover, Gorin's blade strikes his neck. There is a flash, and in a shower of sparks the rabbit disappears.

The shock of the vicious attack
leaves you trembling.
TURN to 5.

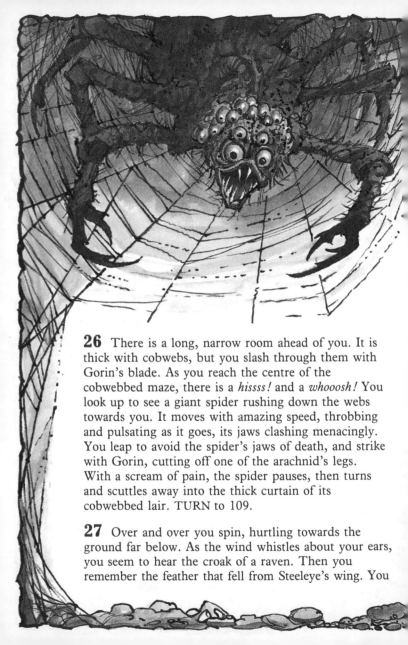

26 There is a long, narrow room ahead of you. It is thick with cobwebs, but you slash through them with Gorin's blade. As you reach the centre of the cobwebbed maze, there is a *hissss!* and a *whooosh!* You look up to see a giant spider rushing down the webs towards you. It moves with amazing speed, throbbing and pulsating as it goes, its jaws clashing menacingly. You leap to avoid the spider's jaws of death, and strike with Gorin, cutting off one of the arachnid's legs. With a scream of pain, the spider pauses, then turns and scuttles away into the thick curtain of its cobwebbed lair. TURN to 109.

27 Over and over you spin, hurtling towards the ground far below. As the wind whistles about your ears, you seem to hear the croak of a raven. Then you remember the feather that fell from Steeleye's wing. You

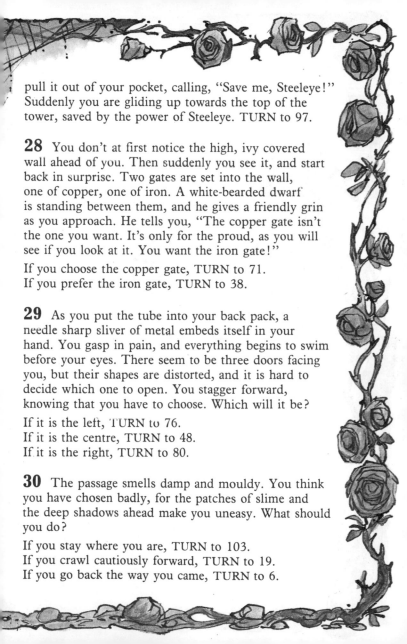

pull it out of your pocket, calling, "Save me, Steeleye!"
Suddenly you are gliding up towards the top of the
tower, saved by the power of Steeleye. TURN to 97.

28 You don't at first notice the high, ivy covered
wall ahead of you. Then suddenly you see it, and start
back in surprise. Two gates are set into the wall,
one of copper, one of iron. A white-bearded dwarf
is standing between them, and he gives a friendly grin
as you approach. He tells you, "The copper gate isn't
the one you want. It's only for the proud, as you will
see if you look at it. You want the iron gate!"

If you choose the copper gate, TURN to 71.
If you prefer the iron gate, TURN to 38.

29 As you put the tube into your back pack, a
needle sharp sliver of metal embeds itself in your
hand. You gasp in pain, and everything begins to swim
before your eyes. There seem to be three doors facing
you, but their shapes are distorted, and it is hard to
decide which one to open. You stagger forward,
knowing that you have to choose. Which will it be?

If it is the left, TURN to 76.
If it is the centre, TURN to 48.
If it is the right, TURN to 80.

30 The passage smells damp and mouldy. You think
you have chosen badly, for the patches of slime and
the deep shadows ahead make you uneasy. What should
you do?

If you stay where you are, TURN to 103.
If you crawl cautiously forward, TURN to 19.
If you go back the way you came, TURN to 6.

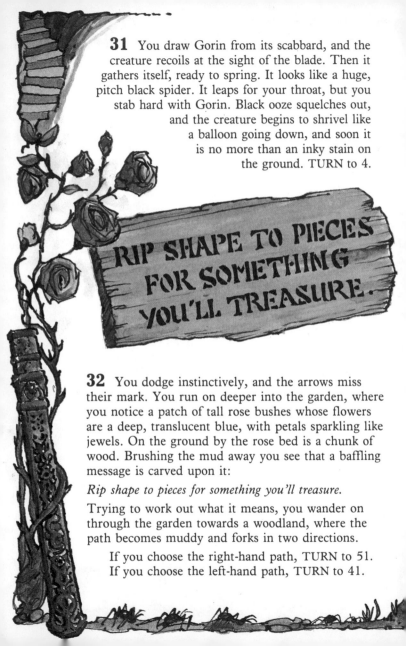

31 You draw Gorin from its scabbard, and the creature recoils at the sight of the blade. Then it gathers itself, ready to spring. It looks like a huge, pitch black spider. It leaps for your throat, but you stab hard with Gorin. Black ooze squelches out, and the creature begins to shrivel like a balloon going down, and soon it is no more than an inky stain on the ground. TURN to 4.

RIP SHAPE TO PIECES FOR SOMETHING YOU'LL TREASURE.

32 You dodge instinctively, and the arrows miss their mark. You run on deeper into the garden, where you notice a patch of tall rose bushes whose flowers are a deep, translucent blue, with petals sparkling like jewels. On the ground by the rose bed is a chunk of wood. Brushing the mud away you see that a baffling message is carved upon it:

Rip shape to pieces for something you'll treasure.

Trying to work out what it means, you wander on through the garden towards a woodland, where the path becomes muddy and forks in two directions.

If you choose the right-hand path, TURN to 51.
If you choose the left-hand path, TURN to 41.

33 You race on up the stairs and discover that they curve up to a wide landing. Ahead of you are two leather padded doors. To left and right of the doors are more flights of stairs. You make your choice.

The left flight leads to 10.
The left door leads to 58.
The right door leads to 113.
The right flight leads to 13.

34 Leaving the echo of the voices behind, you head along the passage. It leads up a narrow spiral staircase and into a high-domed chamber, filled with a sound of rustling. The whole room quivers with life. As your eyes get used to the gloom, you perceive something brown and huge in the middle of the chamber. TURN to 17.

35 The lily pads are broad, and they easily bear your weight. The calls of invisible water fowl sound mournfully in your ears. The Unicorn has disappeared, and the far shore of the lake is distant and shrouded in mist. But, as you cross the water, the mist starts to clear and you begin to make out the shape of a great castle ahead of you. TURN to 87.

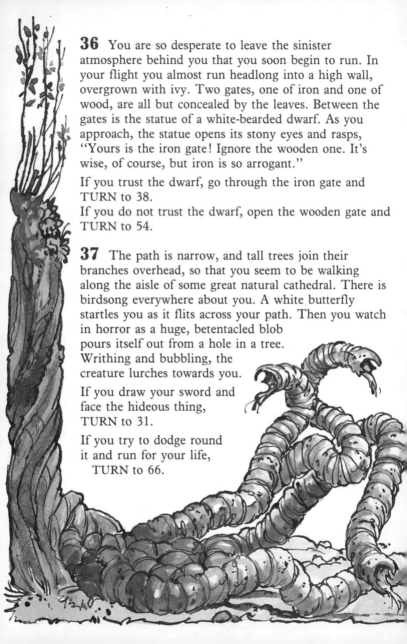

36 You are so desperate to leave the sinister atmosphere behind you that you soon begin to run. In your flight you almost run headlong into a high wall, overgrown with ivy. Two gates, one of iron and one of wood, are all but concealed by the leaves. Between the gates is the statue of a white-bearded dwarf. As you approach, the statue opens its stony eyes and rasps, "Yours is the iron gate! Ignore the wooden one. It's wise, of course, but iron is so arrogant."

If you trust the dwarf, go through the iron gate and TURN to 38.

If you do not trust the dwarf, open the wooden gate and TURN to 54.

37 The path is narrow, and tall trees join their branches overhead, so that you seem to be walking along the aisle of some great natural cathedral. There is birdsong everywhere about you. A white butterfly startles you as it flits across your path. Then you watch in horror as a huge, betentacled blob pours itself out from a hole in a tree. Writhing and bubbling, the creature lurches towards you.

If you draw your sword and face the hideous thing, TURN to 31.

If you try to dodge round it and run for your life, TURN to 66.

38 You look at the iron gate and see the words *'The arrogant'* woven into its decoration. Wondering what it means, you push the gate open and pass into a garden that lies beyond it. Soon your path is blocked by a dense hedge of roses.

If you go right, TURN to 25.
If you go left, TURN to 49.

39 A green, otter-like creature has you in its grip, but its eyes are gentle and your fears depart. The creature begins to make strange, high pitched sounds. It seems to be whistling a message to you:

FNNC KTBJ, GDQN! SGD FQDDMR VHKK ZKVZXR AD NM XNTQ RHCD.

It then darts away into the marsh and you continue your quest. TURN to 12.

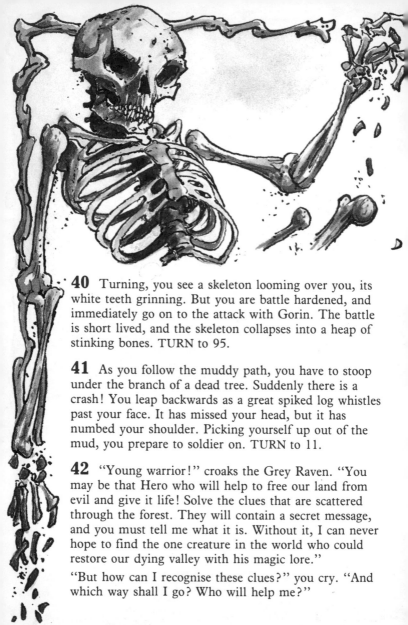

40 Turning, you see a skeleton looming over you, its white teeth grinning. But you are battle hardened, and immediately go on to the attack with Gorin. The battle is short lived, and the skeleton collapses into a heap of stinking bones. TURN to 95.

41 As you follow the muddy path, you have to stoop under the branch of a dead tree. Suddenly there is a crash! You leap backwards as a great spiked log whistles past your face. It has missed your head, but it has numbed your shoulder. Picking yourself up out of the mud, you prepare to soldier on. TURN to 11.

42 "Young warrior!" croaks the Grey Raven. "You may be that Hero who will help to free our land from evil and give it life! Solve the clues that are scattered through the forest. They will contain a secret message, and you must tell me what it is. Without it, I can never hope to find the one creature in the world who could restore our dying valley with his magic lore."

"But how can I recognise these clues?" you cry. "And which way shall I go? Who will help me?"

"The enchanted sword called Gorin will protect you on your quest," the Raven answers. "Gorin is waiting for you now, if you care to take him from his resting place beneath this oak tree. And creatures of the forest will meet you on your way. Some will help, but others will be your enemies. My brothers will keep you on the right path when choices have to be made. Look for their signs. I can tell you no more," the Raven says, opening his wings and beginning to fly away, "but read the scroll I leave you. And take Gorin!"

As the great bird circles overhead, he drops a parchment scroll at your feet. A feather from his powerful wings flutters after it.

You fall to your knees and there, hidden beneath the gnarled root of the oak tree, you see Gorin in its great leather scabbard. Hastily strapping it round your waist, you pick up the scroll and the feather. You begin walking towards the gloomy forest. TURN to 9.

43 On the bronze gate are engraved the words, *'The good.'* You raise the latch, push the gate open, and walk through. You find yourself in a formal garden, and the path you are on leads directly to a bed of rose bushes. The path divides when it reaches the rose bed.

If you go left round the rose bed, TURN to 63.
If you go right round the rose bed, TURN to 49.

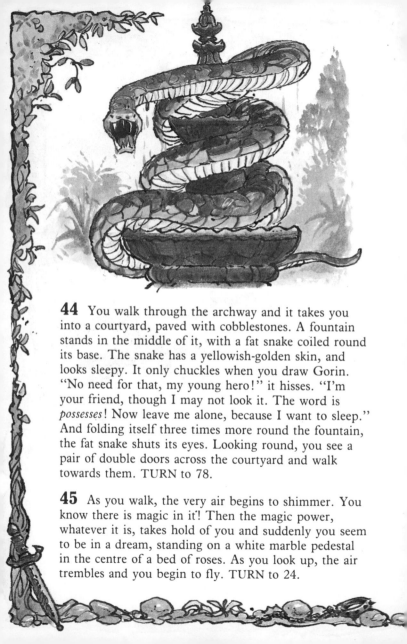

44 You walk through the archway and it takes you into a courtyard, paved with cobblestones. A fountain stands in the middle of it, with a fat snake coiled round its base. The snake has a yellowish-golden skin, and looks sleepy. It only chuckles when you draw Gorin. "No need for that, my young hero!" it hisses. "I'm your friend, though I may not look it. The word is *possesses*! Now leave me alone, because I want to sleep." And folding itself three times more round the fountain, the fat snake shuts its eyes. Looking round, you see a pair of double doors across the courtyard and walk towards them. TURN to 78.

45 As you walk, the very air begins to shimmer. You know there is magic in it! Then the magic power, whatever it is, takes hold of you and suddenly you seem to be in a dream, standing on a white marble pedestal in the centre of a bed of roses. As you look up, the air trembles and you begin to fly. TURN to 24.

46 You are walking along the path when, with a blood-chilling yell, a Chimera leaps upon you. It has a lion's head, a serpent's tail, and the body of a goat. Its sharp hooves drum on your chest, and its tail stings you again and again. You stab from below with Gorin, and gradually the terrifying beast melts away into the air. You walk on with a shudder.
TURN to 3.

47 The desk seems to be inviting you to open it! Inside it, you find a sealed lead tube. Is there some danger inside it? Or could it conceal a clue to the lost magic?

If you open it, TURN to 18.
If you decide to take it with you unopened, TURN to 29.

48 Once inside the doorway, your eyes again see everything clearly. There are no more distorted shapes and changing patterns. You are in a high chamber, dark and gloomy. You jump in alarm at a clanking noise which comes from behind your back. Turning, you see a rusty suit of armour standing at your shoulder.

It groans: *"The ancient, the ancient, the ancient...* I can scarcely – " Whereupon it falls apart with a clatter. You push aside the pieces of iron, and thoughtfully continue with your quest.

If you explore to your left, TURN to 23.
If you explore to your right, TURN to 77.

49 A carpet of soft, downy feathers covers the path you have chosen. It leads round a pond. As you pass by its banks, a huge water beast erupts from the depths. It tries to cripple you by lashing its scaly tail but, choosing your moment carefully, you leap over the thrashing tail. Then you slash downwards with Gorin. The sword's blade is covered with blood, and the water beast no longer has a tail to harm you with!

If you continue along the same path, TURN to 2.
If you go back to find another way, TURN to 5.

50 Out of the blackness comes a warm, green light. You sit up, bewildered yet glad to be alive. Your adventure ends here, but the land still desperately needs your help. TURN to 1 and start again on your quest for the lost magic. Better luck this time.

51 The muddy path twists and turns, winding its way between trees that are almost hidden by thickets of pale bramble bushes with huge, spiky thorns. But one tree is clearly visible, and you notice a white arrow cut deep into the bark of its trunk.

If you follow the direction of the arrow, TURN to 11.
If you go the other way, TURN to 3.

52 Stepping on to dry land, you walk towards the castle gateway. Barring your path is a creature with an eagle's head and a lion's body. The mighty Gryphon looks you up and down and then utters, in a deep voice, "Pass, friend!" Beyond the gateway to your left is a wooden door. To your right is a passage.

If you go through the door, TURN to 86.
If you go down the passage, TURN to 30.

53 Brambles clutch at your legs as you push your way along the narrow path. Ahead, you see a patch of blackness on the dark forest floor. It could be a deep pit, or a pool, or a swamp! You cannot tell what it is!

Are you going to leap over it? Then TURN to 79.
Are you going to edge round it? Then TURN to 82.

54 The wooden gate has the words *'The wise'* painted on it. It swings open with a creak, and you see beyond it into a rose garden. You walk in, but soon find that a dense hedge is barring your way forward, and you will have to follow the path round it either by the left or by the right.

If you go to the right, TURN to 49.
If you go to the left, TURN to 63.

55 You thud against some kind of slope, then slither further down into the darkness. You find that you have landed against a clump of thorny bushes. TURN to 67.

56 You begin to walk over slabs of a rich, dull metal. There is a flurry of wings, but you cannot see what bird has flown by you. Some words are engraved on one of the slabs, and you rub away the tarnish that obscures the letters. Where you have cleaned the metal, it gleams in the sunlight. At last you read:

In part, gold encloses the secret. A precious description of the creature is hiding here.

You walk on towards a grove of saplings that marks the beginning of a wood. Your senses begin to tingle as you walk into the grove. TURN to 106.

57 Your speed is your enemy, for you trip and fall headlong. To your horror, the ground gives way, sending you falling down into a pit of darkness. TURN to 107.

58 The door creaks open on its rusty hinges. You are in a small room, and the feeling of claustrophobia makes you want to rush out again. Then, as you turn to leave, you see an old desk in a corner. TURN to 47.

59 You wriggle through a tiny window set high in the wall of the chamber. "Be brave!" cries the tree spirit, as you clamber through and begin to climb up the ivy on the outside wall of the castle, towards the roof. A bat suddenly bursts out of a cranny in the stonework.

You try to keep your grip, but the flurry of its wings has made you lose your balance. Slowly you begin to topple towards the courtyard far below. TURN to 27.

60 The grass on the path soon becomes tired and colourless. It takes you to a high garden wall set with two gates, one of wood and the other of bronze. Sitting between the gates is a white-bearded dwarf. As you approach, he croaks these words: "The wooden gate is best. Bronze is good, but it isn't the one you want."

If you follow the dwarf's advice, TURN to 54.
If you ignore his warning, TURN to 43.

61 The chamber seems to stretch endlessly before you. Flecks of white plaster fall from the crumbling ceiling. In the dust are tiny arrow marks, because a bird has been hopping there along the chamber floor. As you walk, an ominous rumbling fills the air and you know that danger is very close.

If you run down the room, TURN to 57.
If you walk on calmly, TURN to 91.

62 *Splat!* At your feet lands a rubbery creature, something like a frog. Its throat is pulsing and vibrating, and you realise it is trying to give you a message. This is what you hear:

"EHT ERUTAERC SI EHT YEK"

The strange messenger leaves you, hopping and bounding as it skims away across the water.

If you follow it, TURN to 52.
If you go your own way, TURN to 20.

63 As you wander on through the garden, you are struck by the sight of a huge bird bath, made of white marble. You peer over its lip and look into the sparkling water it holds. Then a great tentacle snakes out and grabs you by the left wrist. Quick as a flash, you draw Gorin, for you know that you must free yourself before you are pulled down into the water. You slash out with the sword, and there is a spurt of blood. TURN to 2.

64 A joyous burst of birdsong greets you as you step from the last lily pad on to the rocky shore near the castle gate. High up on a dead tree nearby perches an Eagle. It fixes its piercing eye upon you.

"I am the Guardian of the Gate," it declares. "None may enter without my leave."

"I am a Hero in search of the heart of this land," you answer. "I seek it within the castle."

"Pass in peace!" the Eagle replies solemnly, leaving you to walk through the archway. "I give you my name, at least."

Before you is a flight of worn stone steps, and, on your right, a solid iron-bound door.

If you choose to open the door, TURN to 86.
If you climb the steps, TURN to 105.

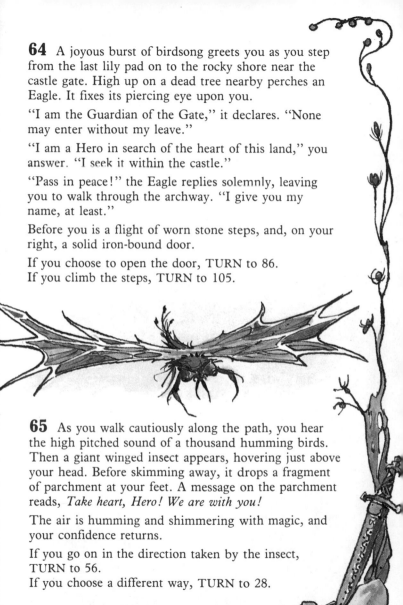

65 As you walk cautiously along the path, you hear the high pitched sound of a thousand humming birds. Then a giant winged insect appears, hovering just above your head. Before skimming away, it drops a fragment of parchment at your feet. A message on the parchment reads, *Take heart, Hero! We are with you!*

The air is humming and shimmering with magic, and your confidence returns.

If you go on in the direction taken by the insect, TURN to 56.
If you choose a different way, TURN to 28.

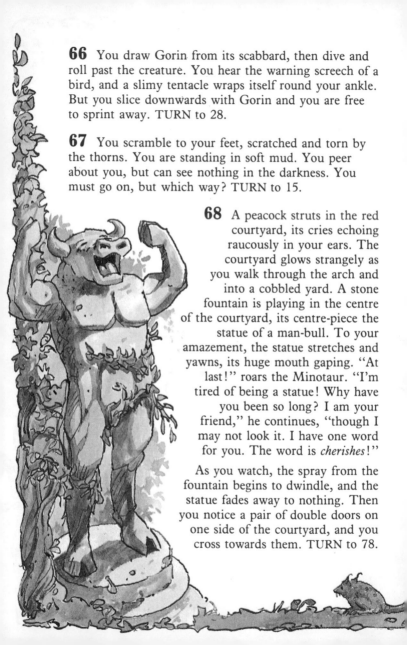

66 You draw Gorin from its scabbard, then dive and roll past the creature. You hear the warning screech of a bird, and a slimy tentacle wraps itself round your ankle. But you slice downwards with Gorin and you are free to sprint away. TURN to 28.

67 You scramble to your feet, scratched and torn by the thorns. You are standing in soft mud. You peer about you, but can see nothing in the darkness. You must go on, but which way? TURN to 15.

68 A peacock struts in the red courtyard, its cries echoing raucously in your ears. The courtyard glows strangely as you walk through the arch and into a cobbled yard. A stone fountain is playing in the centre of the courtyard, its centre-piece the statue of a man-bull. To your amazement, the statue stretches and yawns, its huge mouth gaping. "At last!" roars the Minotaur. "I'm tired of being a statue! Why have you been so long? I am your friend," he continues, "though I may not look it. I have one word for you. The word is *cherishes*!"

As you watch, the spray from the fountain begins to dwindle, and the statue fades away to nothing. Then you notice a pair of double doors on one side of the courtyard, and you cross towards them. TURN to 78.

69 A damp hero continues the quest, wetter but wiser. You jump from lily pad to lily pad, aiming to reach the misty shore ahead. Gradually the mist disperses to reveal the outline of a castle, and you realise that the lake is really a moat. Then the lily pad you are standing on begins to split in two.

If you go with the left half, TURN to 16.
If you go with the right half, TURN to 116.

70 Quickly and lightly, you step from pad to pad. The mists that hide the shore ahead begin to lift, and you can just make out the shape of a great castle. You realise that the lake is really a moat. TURN to 62.

71 You look at the copper gate, and see the words *'The proud'* painted in green on it. You push the gate open and pass through into a formal garden. The sound of birdsong is deafening, though you can see no birds. Ahead of you is a dense hedge of roses. It is blocking the way ahead, so you have to go round it.

If you go round it to the right, TURN to 25.
If you go round it to the left, TURN to 49.

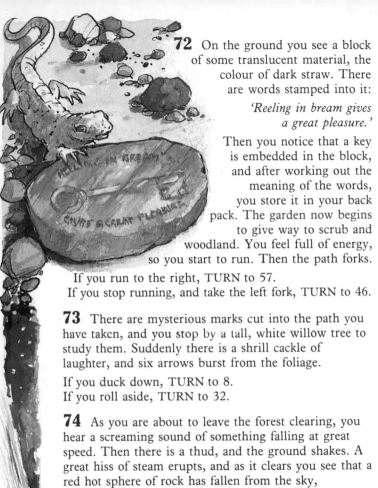

72 On the ground you see a block of some translucent material, the colour of dark straw. There are words stamped into it:

'Reeling in bream gives a great pleasure.'

Then you notice that a key is embedded in the block, and after working out the meaning of the words, you store it in your back pack. The garden now begins to give way to scrub and woodland. You feel full of energy, so you start to run. Then the path forks.

If you run to the right, TURN to 57.
If you stop running, and take the left fork, TURN to 46.

73 There are mysterious marks cut into the path you have taken, and you stop by a tall, white willow tree to study them. Suddenly there is a shrill cackle of laughter, and six arrows burst from the foliage.

If you duck down, TURN to 8.
If you roll aside, TURN to 32.

74 As you are about to leave the forest clearing, you hear a screaming sound of something falling at great speed. Then there is a thud, and the ground shakes. A great hiss of steam erupts, and as it clears you see that a red hot sphere of rock has fallen from the sky, embedding itself deeply into the ground. You investigate, but the meteorite can tell you nothing, so you walk on along the path. TURN to 7.

75 It leads to a narrow spiral staircase, which winds upwards to a high-domed chamber that seems to quiver with life. There is a rustling sound. It is the noise of birds in leafy branches. As your eyes become accustomed to the gloom, you realise that a dark brown figure is standing in the middle of the chamber. TURN to 17.

76 Through the doorway, and passing along the landing, you reach a dark and gloomy chamber where ancient suits of armour line the walls. You gaze at them, and realise with a shock that one of them is gazing back at you. *"The secret, the secret, the secret – "* it groans, then collapses into a heap of bands, rivets and plates.

If you want to explore the chamber by going right, TURN to 23.
If you want to explore the chamber by going left, TURN to 77.

77 You make your way along the chamber, wondering what the next danger will be. You soon find out! A great white bat comes swooping down, aiming for your throat, and you have to dive for the ground to avoid its cruel fangs. To your horror, the floorboards collapse under your weight, and you are falling into what seems like endless night. TURN to 55.

78 The doors are made of mahogany, and they open smoothly at a push. A staircase lies behind them, and boldly you make your way up into the darkness above. Suddenly, a shower of wriggling creatures falls upon your head. Hundreds of tiny, luminous white snakes are writhing all over your body. You try to shake them off, but without success. Then you draw Gorin, and as the mighty sword hisses from its scabbard the snakes retreat and disappear into the gloom. TURN to 33.

79 Taking a short run-up, you leap over the dark patch on the forest floor. There is a hideous bubbling sound, and the patch erupts into the air. Some of its primordial ooze splashes on your legs. You tuck and roll, hitting the ground hard on the far side of the bubbling blackness, but livid patches mark the places where the stuff touched your skin.

If you pause for a while to tend your wound,
TURN to 36.
If you hurry on, TURN to 12.

80 Slowly the mist clears from your eyes, and you find yourself leaning against the wall of a high chamber, dark and gloomy. Suits of armour stand in niches along the walls, and, as you look at them, one cries out to you in a creaking voice: *"The mighty, the mighty, the mighty – "* Then it falls to pieces at your feet.

If you go exploring to your right, TURN to 77.
If you go up the stairs to your left, TURN to 33.

81 The passage leads up a wide spiral staircase that follows the inside wall of a high tower. Hugging the wall for fear of falling, you climb up. At last you reach a high-domed chamber that seems to be quivering with life. As your eyes get used to the gloom, you realise that a thick-set figure stands in the very centre of the chamber. TURN to 17.

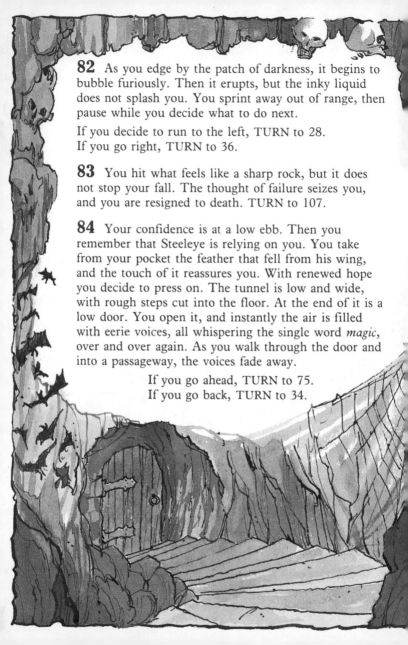

82 As you edge by the patch of darkness, it begins to bubble furiously. Then it erupts, but the inky liquid does not splash you. You sprint away out of range, then pause while you decide what to do next.

If you decide to run to the left, TURN to 28.
If you go right, TURN to 36.

83 You hit what feels like a sharp rock, but it does not stop your fall. The thought of failure seizes you, and you are resigned to death. TURN to 107.

84 Your confidence is at a low ebb. Then you remember that Steeleye is relying on you. You take from your pocket the feather that fell from his wing, and the touch of it reassures you. With renewed hope you decide to press on. The tunnel is low and wide, with rough steps cut into the floor. At the end of it is a low door. You open it, and instantly the air is filled with eerie voices, all whispering the single word *magic*, over and over again. As you walk through the door and into a passageway, the voices fade away.

If you go ahead, TURN to 75.
If you go back, TURN to 34.

85 Apart from the amulet, there is no sign of the creature who attacked you. On an impulse, you pick up the amulet and study it. On one side it is inscribed with the words, *Trust Steeleye's brothers*. On the other side is written the message, *Thrice armour speaks key*. You put the amulet in your back pack and press on into the darkness. Just round the next corner, you come upon a red door. Opening it, you see that it leads into a red courtyard. But next to the door is an amber coloured archway.

If you choose the red door, TURN to 68.
If you choose the amber archway, TURN to 44.

86 You push the door, and as it opens you see that a message is carved into the wood. It reads: *The amulet rings true!* Then the words are gone. You rub your eyes in disbelief. Did you dream the words? You shut the heavy door behind you, and find yourself facing three sets of stairs, but you cannot see what lies beyond them.

If you go up set one, TURN to 19.
If you take set two, TURN to 6.
If you go down set three, TURN to 93.

87 The dangers are not yet over! Out of the water comes the head and long neck of a huge sea beast. It gropes blindly, trying to clutch you. But the sunlight glints on the bright blade of Gorin, and as the sword flashes fire the beast gives a shudder and disappears once more into the water. TURN to 64.

88 Your chosen route takes you into a high chamber, dark and gloomy. There is a fluttering at the window, as a bird beats its wings against the grimy panes of glass. Your heart is in your mouth at the sound of iron clanking behind you. Turning quickly, you find a suit of rusty armour at your back. *"The lost, the lost, the lost –"* it groans, then falls to pieces with a great clatter.

If you go on through the chamber to your left, TURN to 77.
If you press on to the right, TURN to 61.

89 You pick up the talisman left by the ghost. On one side are the words, *Trust Steeleye's brothers*, and on the other, written in a circle, is a message: *Three times armour says key*. You put the talisman in your back pack, and go on into the darkness. Round the next corner are two archways, and through each of them you can see a courtyard and a fountain. But one view is bathed in a green light, and the other glows pale blue.

If you choose the green courtyard, TURN to 110.
If you choose the blue courtyard, TURN to 100.

90 The amulet glows with a pale light, and, hesitantly, you pick it up and examine it. On one side are the words, *Trust Steeleye's brothers*. The other side has the phrase, *Armour's thrice spoken key*. You cram the amulet into your back pack, and walk on. As you turn the next corner, there are two archways facing you. Through one arch you can see the light blue glow of a castle courtyard. Through the other is the same view, but the glow is a warm amber.

If you choose amber, TURN to 44.
If you choose blue, TURN to 100.

91 Bravely you walk onwards, aware of an anxious cheeping noise that comes from high in the vaulted ceiling. But huge blocks of stone are falling from above. One of the stones strikes you a glancing blow, and you fall over. To your horror, the floor collapses under you, and you are tumbling down into the darkness below. TURN to 107.

92 Climbing up the slippery slope to the tunnel entrance is not easy, nor is the way along the tunnel itself. But at last you reach a trapdoor, and push up its heavy lid. At once you hear the sound of voices, all whispering the same word: *enchantment, enchantment*. Then the voices die away. You look around and discover that you are in a corridor.

If you go left, TURN to 94.
If you go right, TURN to 75.

93 From far away, it seems, there comes the lonely cry of an anxious bird. You feel a sudden chill, and a smell of decay from the vault at the foot of the steps. Your scalp tingles, but you step bravely into the vault, your fingers tightening round Gorin. You sense an attack. It comes from behind, as bony fingers fasten about your neck. TURN to 40.

94 The corridor leads upwards in a spiral that runs round the inside wall of a tall tower. You follow eagerly, until you reach a high-domed chamber. The whole room seems to be quivering with life, and as your eyes become used to the gloom you are aware of a powerful figure in the middle of the floor. TURN to 17.

95 Among the scattered bones lies an antique golden amulet. You pick it up and discover an inscription on it that reads, *Armour sounds thrice important*. You store the amulet away and continue on. Ahead are two doors, and you open them both. One is coloured red, and it leads through into a red courtyard. The other is coloured blue, and would take you into an identical blue courtyard.

If you choose to go through the red door, TURN to 68.
If you choose to go through the blue door, TURN to 102.

96 Your chosen route takes you to a large chamber lined with rusty suits of armour. Curious, you begin to examine them, but stiffen as an iron fist suddenly clamps your shoulder. You turn your head to discover that one of the suits of armour has you in its grip! The armour speaks to you, groaning the words, *"The old, the old, the old – "* Then it collapses into a pile of rusty metal. You back away from the heap, and decide to move on.

To go down the chamber to your right,

TURN to 61.

To go down the chamber to your left,

TURN to 77.

97 You circle the tower and manage to land on its roof. There, cut into one of the battlements, is a final message. *Your quest is over, Hero!* it reads. *Shout out your message, and wait for help to set you on your journey home.*

You look up, and there is Steeleye hovering above you. Excited now, you shout out the message he has waited for so long to hear. Then he speeds away, croaking his thanks, to find the creature who can tell him how to restore the heart beat of his land. As he disappears from your sight, the air around you is filled with the sound of beating wings, and a giant butterfly of all the rainbow's colours lands by your side. It folds its wings and offers you its back to take you from the tower. TURN to 117.

98 Taking a deep breath, you dive into the cold, dark water. As you strike for the surface, something grabs you, pulling you down into the murky depths. You feel hundreds of little teeth biting your body, and it feels as though you are being stabbed by pins and needles. But you kick down strongly when your feet touch bottom, and this time you manage to surface. Gasping for breath, you crawl out of the water by scrambling on to one of the huge lily pads that form a path of stepping stones across the lake. TURN to 69.

99 The path you have taken passes beneath a willow tree. Pushing its branches aside, you sense danger. Then you hear the whine of an arrow winging its way towards you. TURN to 8.

100 You walk into the courtyard. Ahead of you is a bubbling fountain, and perched on its rim sits a boy, strangely dressed in a green shirt and wrinkled stockings. There is a red feather stuck in his tall green hat. As you draw near, he looks up and smiles at you, but a tear is rolling down his cheek. "At last!" he sobs. "I have waited so long! The Great Raven told me to give you a word. I chose *keeps*." He then points across the courtyard to a set of double doors. You go towards them. TURN to 78.

101 The grassy path slopes down into a shallow depression in the ground. In the centre of the hollow is a massive slab of granite, and on the rock in glowing green letters is the message, ELPMISSIHTEBLLIWSEULCLLATON. TURN to 21.

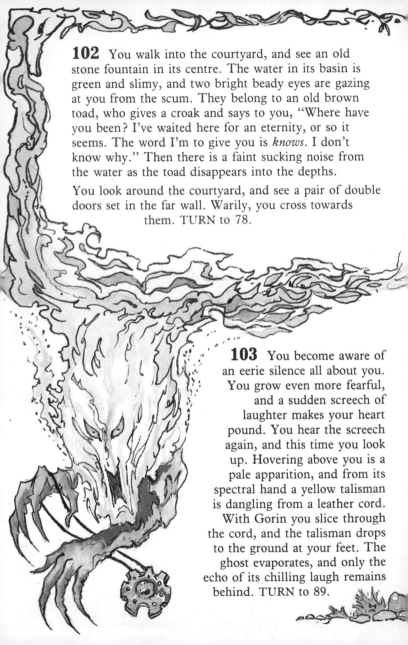

102 You walk into the courtyard, and see an old stone fountain in its centre. The water in its basin is green and slimy, and two bright beady eyes are gazing at you from the scum. They belong to an old brown toad, who gives a croak and says to you, "Where have you been? I've waited here for an eternity, or so it seems. The word I'm to give you is *knows*. I don't know why." Then there is a faint sucking noise from the water as the toad disappears into the depths.

You look around the courtyard, and see a pair of double doors set in the far wall. Warily, you cross towards them. TURN to 78.

103 You become aware of an eerie silence all about you. You grow even more fearful, and a sudden screech of laughter makes your heart pound. You hear the screech again, and this time you look up. Hovering above you is a pale apparition, and from its spectral hand a yellow talisman is dangling from a leather cord. With Gorin you slice through the cord, and the talisman drops to the ground at your feet. The ghost evaporates, and only the echo of its chilling laugh remains behind. TURN to 89.

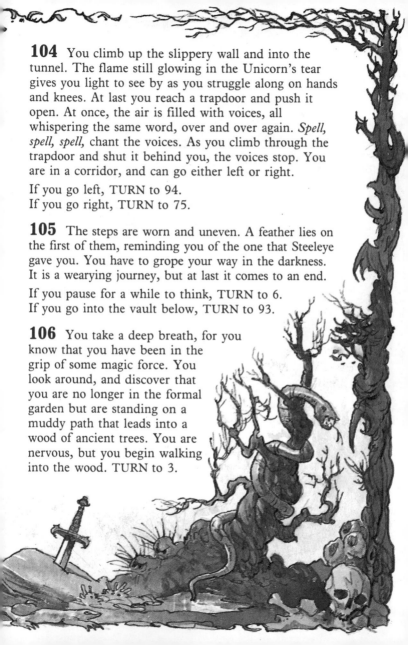

104 You climb up the slippery wall and into the tunnel. The flame still glowing in the Unicorn's tear gives you light to see by as you struggle along on hands and knees. At last you reach a trapdoor and push it open. At once, the air is filled with voices, all whispering the same word, over and over again. *Spell, spell, spell,* chant the voices. As you climb through the trapdoor and shut it behind you, the voices stop. You are in a corridor, and can go either left or right.

If you go left, TURN to 94.
If you go right, TURN to 75.

105 The steps are worn and uneven. A feather lies on the first of them, reminding you of the one that Steeleye gave you. You have to grope your way in the darkness. It is a wearying journey, but at last it comes to an end.

If you pause for a while to think, TURN to 6.
If you go into the vault below, TURN to 93.

106 You take a deep breath, for you know that you have been in the grip of some magic force. You look around, and discover that you are no longer in the formal garden but are standing on a muddy path that leads into a wood of ancient trees. You are nervous, but you begin walking into the wood. TURN to 3.

107 You land with a thud on a thick layer of straw that smells of a wild beast! You sense something wild and hungry lurking there in the darkness. You draw Gorin, in case you have to fight for your life. Then there is a snarl, and the smell of beast is even stronger. You sense, rather than see, the leap when it comes and a huge black cat is upon you, slashing at you with its talons and trying to tear your neck with its sabre teeth. You cannot wield Gorin like a sword, but you can use it as a dagger. Again and again in the black darkness you stab desperately at the soft underbelly of the animal until, howling with pain, it drags itself off you and crawls away into its hidden lair. TURN to 15.

108 The tunnel leads to a vertical shaft, with stone pegs set in its wall at regular intervals. You climb up them until you reach a heavy trapdoor, which pushes open without difficulty. As you climb through it into a passageway, the air suddenly fills with the sound of voices, all whispering the same word over and over again: *lore, lore, lore.* As you close the trapdoor, the voices fade away.

If you go left along the passage, TURN to 34.
If you go right, TURN to 81.

109 Beyond the cobwebs, the room is piled high with rubbish. You walk the length of the room until you spy a door, almost hidden by a faded tapestry showing bees gathering honey. You seem to hear the bees speaking to you in a low pitched hum. But the queen is telling you to go through the door and turn left, while the workers are telling you to go through the door and turn right.

If you listen to the queen bee, TURN to 96.
If you listen to the worker bees, TURN to 88.

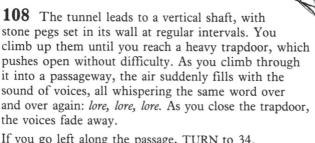

110 You pass through the archway into the courtyard, at whose centre is a bubbling fountain. Sitting on the rim of the stonework is a boy, dressed in shades of green, with a single red feather in his hat. He is holding his head in his hands, but looks up as you approach.

"I am not of your world," he sighs, "but I have waited for you for so long. I have a word to give you. It is *retains*." He smiles faintly, then fades from sight.

Looking around the courtyard, you see a set of double doors in the far wall, and cross over to them.
TURN to 78.

111 You try to keep your balance, then begin clutching frantically at the bare stone, hoping to find a hand hold. But you are falling, and a strange sense of peace enfolds you as you realise you are going to die.
TURN to 27.

112 You clamber up the wall, which is slippery with moss, and manage to haul yourself into the tunnel. Crawling along it is hard work, but at last you reach a trapdoor and push it open. At once the air is filled with voices, all whispering the same word over and over again: *sorcery, sorcery, sorcery.*

As you shut the trapdoor, the voices fade away. Puzzled, you walk along a corridor that leads to two more passages.

If you take the wider passage, TURN to 34.
If you take the narrower passage, TURN to 81.

113 The door creaks open on its rusted hinges, and you walk into a small, airless room. It is so stuffy that your one thought is to get out again. Then you see an oak desk standing against the wall. It is the only object in the room not covered by a thick layer of white dust. Your curiosity is aroused, and you go over to it. TURN to 47.

114 You are lifted up on to the King's gnarled old shoulders, where a white dove is nestling, and you are just able to reach a small window set high in the wall of the chamber. You scramble out on to a narrow ledge, and find yourself high above the courtyard of the castle. You begin to climb upwards to the top of the tower, but your foot slips, and you lose your grip. TURN to 111.

115 The noble beast fixes you with a gaze of terrifying power, yet its speech is gentle. "The land is dying, young Hero!" it says. "You alone could save it, if you are strong and brave. Its wound needs tending. That without colour spells danger! Trust the Brothers of the Rainbow. Trust Gorin. Trust Steeleye's words. If you are wise and brave, and have luck on your side, the heart of the land may beat again. Go now, across the lake. But first, I give you my protection."

A great tear rolls down the Unicorn's green muzzle. "Cup your hands and catch it!" he cries. To your surprise, the tear is solid and warm in the palm of your hand.

You prepare to walk on over the lily pads which are spread like stepping stones leading in two separate paths across the water.

If you choose the first lily pad path, TURN to 35.
If you choose the second, TURN to 70.
If you choose to swim, TURN to 98.

116 At last you set foot on land again, and you begin climbing towards the castle gate. But there is a sudden grumbling and rumbling, and out of the shadows a brown grizzly Bear lumbers up to you.

"I am the Guardian of the Gate!" it growls. "State your business and be gone!"

"I'm looking for the heart of the land," you reply cautiously. "I believe it lies in the castle."

"I know nothing about that," answers the Bear, sniffing you all over. "But you smell as if you mean no harm! Pass friend."

The Bear points out your way into the castle. This proves to be a small stone porch, from which two passages strike out.

If you take the right-hand passage, TURN to 22.
If you take the left-hand passage, TURN to 30.

117 You feel a sudden tiredness, and are glad to climb on to the butterfly's back. He takes to the air, hovers for a moment, then flies with tremendous speed towards the mountain pass through which you came when first you journeyed to the valley.

If you are the Hero of Destiny, then you are flying above a valley that will soon be restored to life by the Spring of Joy, and in your mind's eye you can see the sparkle of the enchanted stream as it dances in the sunshine. In your imagination, the forest above which you are riding is fresh and green, carpeted with bluebells. But you have reached the mountains, and the valley is already lost to your sight. The butterfly sets you down gently and, as you turn to thank him, his colours fade away until he dissolves like any rainbow on a day of sun and showers.

Your part in the quest for the lost magic is over.

Walt Disney World®

**LADYBIRD BOOKS LTD offer you this
chance of a lifetime 7-day holiday
for you and your family with
TWA and HOWARD JOHNSON HOTELS**

See overleaf for entry form and holiday details

ENTRY FORM

When you have read this book enter the fabulous **Steeleye Competition** by completing **your** message to Steeleye below. Fill in the other entry details and return this form to: **Steeleye Competition, Ladybird Books Ltd, Beeches Road, Loughborough, Leicestershire LE11 2NQ,** to arrive by Monday 30th November 1987.

The message I shouted to Steeleye is...

....

....

....

Name_____ **Age**_____

Address _____

_____

_____ **Post code**_____

Signature of parent or guardian_____

Where book purchased_____

_____

Rules of the competition

1. The competition is open to all children resident in United Kingdom and Eire only who are 12 years old or under at 30th November 1987.
2. The completed entry form must be returned to Ladybird Books Ltd to arrive by Monday 30th November 1987.
3. Any entries which have been filled in incorrectly will, at the discretion of the judges, be disqualified.
4. Persons not eligible to enter the competition are:
(a) Any employee of Ladybird Books Ltd or its subsidiary companies (b) Any employee of Walt Disney Productions (c) Any employee of Trans World Airlines (d) Any employee of Howard Johnson Hotels (e) A judge of the competition (f) Any immediate family of the above.
5. The competition will be judged by a Guest Celebrity on Friday 4th December 1987.
6. The winning entry will be the first all-correct competition form drawn from all those received by the closing date.
7. The winner will be notified by post during the week commencing Monday 7th December 1987.
8. The judges' decision is final and no correspondence will be entered into.
9. No cash alternatives will be offered.
10. The holiday for a family of four (two adults and two children) can be taken at any time during 1988, subject to availability.
11. If you wish to be notified of the winner, please enclose a stamped addressed envelope with your entry.
12. By entering the competition all competitors will be deemed to have agreed to abide by the rules of the competition.